Dedicated to
Guy Bryant who is
making all of my
dreams come true.

Introduction

Does your child have a friend, family member, or class mate who is on the autistic spectrum? Would you like your child or the children in your classroom to understand more about autism? Are you looking for an engaging way to start a dialogue about autism? I wrote this book to solve these challenges.

A is for Autism: A Child's View is a children's picture book in an ABC format. With delightful illustrations, this book teaches typical traits that many people with au tism share. The book uses child-friendlylanguage and is narrated by a 6-year-old with autism. *A is for Autism: A Child's View* provides an entertaining way to start a simple educational discussion about autism.

I invite you to read this story interactively with your child. You can playfully try flapping and rocking with the child in this story. Ask your child to look deeply into your eyes to see if it is uncomfortable for him, too. Encourage discussions of how you or people you love might be like the child in this book. You might compare and contrast how the child in this book is similar or different from a person you know on the spectrum. This book provides wonderful opportunities to discuss how to be a friend of a child with autism. The simple action plan at the conclusion of the book will help give guidance to a child who wants to be a friend of someone on the autistic spectrum.

As a pediatric physical therapist, I work with many children on the spectrum. I often see misinformation about autism and well-meaning, but misguided, attempts to interact with people on the spectrum. I believe knowledge helps break down barriers and encourages kindness and patience. Helping children understand autism at a young age is powerful. Reading this book will change the life of your child and the lives of people on the autistic spectrum that your child meets now and in the future.

A is for Autism
A Child's View

Published by Gotcha Apps, LLC
1904 ½ Williams St.
Valdosta, GA 31602

This book provides general information on autism. It should not be relied upon as recommending or promoting any specific diagnosis or method of treatment. It is not intended as a substitute for medical advice or for direct diagnosis and treatment of autism by a qualified physician. Readers who have questions about autism or its treatment should consult with a physician or other qualified health care professional.

ISBN-13: 978-0-9981567-0-5
ISBN-10: 0-9981567-0-1

Library of Congress Control Number: 2016913966

Cover art and interior artwork by Ikos Ronzkie
Text by Amy E. Sturkey, PT

A is for Autism
A Child's View

written by
Amy E. Sturkey, PT

illustrated by
Ikos Ronzkie

A is for Autism.
No two people are exactly the same.
No two people with autism are exactly the same.
Your friend with autism is probably very different
than me. I bet we are the same in some ways too.
I want to tell you about my life with autism.

B is for Boys.
More boys have autism than girls.

C is for Change.
I don't like change. I like to sit in the same chair,
watch the same videos, wear the same clothes... Oh,
basically I like everything the same, every day.

D is for Don't eat certain foods.
My parents try to help me get better. They tell me
which foods I can eat and which foods I can't eat.
Please do not put those cookies too close to me.
I might snatch them and eat them. If I eat the wrong
foods, watch out! I can get out of control, really fast!
To make things even trickier, I am a very picky
eater. I can count on my fingers the number of foods
I eat. Let's see. I eat chicken nuggets, French Fries,
blue box macaroni, cheese puffs…

E is for Echolalia.
It's kind of like the word echo. Echolalia means
I like to say the words I hear from books or in movies
over and over, and over and over, and over and over.

F is for Flapping.
I flap when I am excited, or happy, or worried, or even a little bored. Flapping my hands feels great, and it helps me calm down. My parents call it a "stim". Flapping is one of my favorite stims, but everyone with autism does their own special stims to help them settle down. Some people with autism press on their ears. Others pick at strings on their socks.
Others hum.

G is for Going to sleep.
I have the hardest time getting to sleep. I hate it
when I wake up in the middle of the night.
Momma has to come and lie down with me to help
me go back to sleep. Sometimes I wake up in the
morning before the sun comes up. I start playing and
making a lot of noise. I'm not sleepy any more.
I can't help it.

H is for Hugging.
I love a good squeeze… but only when I want it.
It really helps me pull myself together. Please don't
think you can come over and hug me anytime.
It has to be my idea.

I is for Ignoring.
I don't mean to ignore you. It is scary for me to look
into your eyes. Is it scary for you? Try it and see!

J is for Jumping.
I could jump all day. Jumping
helps me calm down. I love to jump
really high and really hard.

K is for Keeping and not sharing.
You probably wanted a turn but I don't really
understand how to take turns. I think it should
always be my turn. Isn't everything mine?

L is for Lining up toys.
I like it when my toys are just right.
I get so happy when I line up my cars.
WARNING! I will get really MAD
if you mess them up.

M is for Moody.
If things don't go my way, I can get REALLY mad,
REALLY fast. But don't worry! A few seconds later,
I forget what the fuss was all about. Then I can be
happy and silly. I only think about right now. I forget
yesterday or last week or last year…or even
two minutes ago!

N is for Not Listening.

Sometimes I think so much that I can't hear what you
say, especially if I am moody, if I am in a new place,
or if a lot is going on around me. Even if I hear you,
I might take time to understand what you are saying.
If you talk to me, try counting to 10 to see if I answer
before asking or telling me again. That gives me time
to figure it out. Waiting is hard. You might want
to practice with a friend now.

O is for Obeying.

Sometimes, I am not good at doing what people tell me to do. I want to, but I don't know how to do what you are asking. It is so frustrating. I can skip all day long...but if someone asks me to skip, I don't know how to do it anymore. I do better if you show me what to do instead of all that talking.

P is for Pointing.
I don't understand pointing. I don't know where
to look when people point.

Q is for Quiet.
I used to be very quiet and say nothing at all.
Now I get so excited about things that I talk about
them over and over. I don't notice that you are bored.
Sometimes I ask the same question again and again
just to hear the same answer. I don't notice it
gets on your nerves.

R is for Rocking.
I love to rock my body. It calms me down.
I can rock while sitting or standing.

S is for Spinning.
I love anything that spins.
I love to look at spinning ceiling fans.
I guess it is another one of my "stims."

T is for Talking.
I am not very good at talking the way my friends talk. I don't play pretend very well. I don't easily feel sad when you are sad or happy when you are happy. I don't understand when I hurt your feelings.

U is for Uh-Oh.
I break things a lot. I did not understand until it
was too late that your toy was important to you.
I don't ever say, "Sorry" until my momma tells me.

V is for Volume.
My Volume button is broken. Sometimes I am too quiet, and no one can hear me. Sometimes I am way too LOUD. My daddy says that when everybody gets all quiet, that's when I always YELL! Now let me tell you something funny. I am fine if I am the one yelling, but if you and your friends are too loud around ME, watch out! I can get really upset.

W is for Watching.
I don't know I need to watch when you try to show me something. Seems like I always have trouble watching and learning how to play. I wish I could learn like you do.

X is for eXcitement.
I have autism, but I still have lots of fun.
When I get excited, I am happy from the top of my
head to the bottom of my toes. I forget that I have
ever been sad or mad or scared.

Y is for You.
I really don't know how to be your friend.
I think being friends would be fun if you help me.

Z is for Zip and Zoom.
All this closeness makes me feel scared, so I run
away. If you leave the door open or this book open,
I will zip right out! See you next time!

The end.

If you have a friend who has autism,
I have these 3 simple recommendations:

◇◇◇◇◇◇◇◇◇◇◇◇◇◇◇◇◇◇◇◇◇◇◇◇◇◇◇◇◇◇◇◇

Three-Step Action Plan
1. Be Patient
2. Be Kind
3. Be Understanding

Other offerings by the author:

◇◇

Pediatric Physical Therapy Exercises for Abdominals
for Apple and Android

Pediatric Physical Therapy Exercises for Back Extension
for Apple and Android

Pediatric Physical Therapy Exercises for Back Extension
for Apple and Android

Weekly Blog:
www.pediatricPTexercises.com

Weekly pediatric physical therapy treatment emails:
www.pediatricPTexercises.com

YouTube Channel:
Pediatric Physical Therapy Exercises

Facebook page:
Pediatric Physical Therapy Exercises

About the Illustrator

◇◇◇◇◇◇◇◇◇◇◇◇◇◇◇◇◇◇◇◇◇◇◇◇◇◇◇◇◇◇◇◇◇◇

Ikos Ronzkie is an international graphic designer, book illustrator, and comic artist. She creates fanciful illustrations for advertisements, campaigns, comic books, character designs, book designs and book covers. She has worked as an illustrator with local and international clientele for over 11 years.

She is the illustrator for books including: *What Babies Do*, *What Do I Do Well?*, *The Loosey Goosey Tooth*, *Princess Superhero Antonia*, *The Tooth Fairy* and *Willy Nilly Adventures*.

Her clients include international publishers, dollmakers, comic book writers, authors, and picture book writers. She produces *Bayan ng Biyahero Comics* for the Antipolo Star Newspaper for the Rizal and Metro Manila distribution areas. She previously created *Estudyante Blues* for the Living News and Good Education magazine. Independently, she writes and produces her own comics: *Karit*, *Dalawang Liham*, *Sulsi* and the webcomics *Hilda Intrimitida*. Ronzkie is the co-founder of IKOS Komiks which strives to promote and explore Philippine culture with visual and literary arts. Their creations are dedicated to work inspired by the Philippine history, myths and legends.

◇◇◇◇◇◇◇◇◇◇◇◇◇◇◇◇◇◇◇◇◇◇◇◇◇◇◇◇◇◇◇◇◇◇

Made in the USA
San Bernardino, CA
03 March 2018